Original title:
In the Midst of Melting Moments

Copyright © 2024 Creative Arts Management OÜ
All rights reserved.

Author: Nolan Kingsley
ISBN HARDBACK: 978-9916-90-668-2
ISBN PAPERBACK: 978-9916-90-669-9

A Soft Goodbye

In the twilight's gentle glow,
We whisper secrets soft and low.
The world around begins to fade,
As memories dance in the glade.

Holding tight to moments dear,
We shed both joy and silent fear.
With every breath, a tender sigh,
In the space where goodbyes lie.

Footsteps falter, hearts do ache,
Yet in this path, we dare to take.
With every beat, a love returned,
In softest flames, our hearts have burned.

As nightfall sweeps the sky with care,
We leave behind our whispered prayer.
With heavy hearts, we part our ways,
But love will linger, through the days.

The Impermanence of Light

Flickering candles in the night,
Shadows dance, a fleeting sight.
Whispers carried on the breeze,
Moments lost like falling leaves.

Sunrise paints the skies with gold,
But each dawn, the warmth turns cold.
Fleeting hues in twilight's grasp,
Memories fade, like a whispered gasp.

Hourglass Hymns

Grains of sand swirl and fall,
Echoing time's quiet call.
Each heartbeat marks a new refrain,
Life's symphony, love and pain.

Moments slip through fingers wide,
Cherished dreams we hold inside.
In the stillness, hear the sound,
Of fleeting hours all around.

Mirage of the Present

In the mirror of our mind,
Reflections quickly fall behind.
Here and now, it seems so clear,
Yet, moments vanish, disappear.

Chasing shadows, we collide,
With visions hovering like tide.
Reality's a fleeting mist,
A dance of what we can't resist.

Whirlwind of Wonder

Spinning stars in endless flight,
Curiosity ignites the night.
In our hearts, we crave to know,
The secrets that the cosmos show.

Each question bursts like fireflies,
Illuminating darkened skies.
In the whirlwind, dreams take wing,
And the soul begins to sing.

The Silk of Sunset

Whispers of gold in the fading light,
A canvas painted with gentle delight.
The horizon blushes with hues of flame,
As day bows down, it's never the same.

Soft tendrils of dusk weave through the trees,
A hush settles in with the evening breeze.
In silence, the stars begin to unfold,
While dreams entwine in threads of gold.

Slipping Through Fingers

Time drips like sand from an open hand,
Moments so precious, like grains they stand.
Each tick of the clock echoes clear and loud,
Yet slips away, ungrasped and unbowed.

Memories linger but fade like a sigh,
Whispers of laughter that once danced high.
We chase and we hold, but it dances away,
Life's fleeting moments are never to stay.

Flickers of Radiance

In the dark night, sparks begin to rise,
Flickers of light that dance in the skies.
They twinkle and shimmer, a celestial show,
Guiding the wanderers, kindling the glow.

Heartbeat of the cosmos, pulsing so bright,
Each glimmer a story, a piece of the night.
They weave through the heavens, a tapestry grand,
Illuminating dreams with a delicate hand.

Celestial Drifts

Across the vast void where the soft stardust flows,
Celestial drifts on the night wind blows.
Constellations whisper secrets untold,
While the moon guards wishes like treasures of gold.

Eternal the dance of the planets and spheres,
Waltzing through silence, transcending our years.
In the embrace of the cosmos we trust,
Finding our place in the infinite dust.

Reflections on the Surface

The lake gleams bright, a mirror clear,
Whispers of wind, we draw near.
A glimpse of sky, clouds drift and wane,
In soft ripples, we find our refrain.

Branches dip low, secrets to share,
Each movement, a thought caught in air.
Beneath the calm, the rush of depth,
Life's hidden stories, each breath adept.

The Poetry of Passing Time

Hours like shadows, they fade away,
Moments are ink, the heart's own say.
Every tick sings a silent tune,
Life's tender script beneath the moon.

Seasons shift, the colors blend,
Time is a river, a constant bend.
A glance back yields the sweetest sigh,
In the heart of memories, we never die.

Moments Like Water

Droplets glisten on a sunbeam's trail,
Each a memory, fragile, pale.
They dance like laughter, light and free,
Fleeting instants, like waves at sea.

Rivers run swift, carving their way,
Through valleys deep, where shadows play.
In currents strong, we find our song,
In moments like water, we all belong.

The Fluidity of Life

Life flows gently, a stream's embrace,
In every turn, we find our place.
Like drifting leaves on a winding path,
We weave our stories with love's warm bath.

Tides will rise, and then recede,
Each twist and turn, a brand new seed.
Through every phase, we learn to glide,
In the fluidity of life, we reside.

The Taste of Fleeting Infinity

In the stillness of dusk's embrace,
Colors dance, time leaves no trace.
Moments linger, but then they're gone,
Whispers of past in the twilight's dawn.

A heartbeat echoes, soft and light,
Chasing shadows fading from sight.
Eternity feels just within reach,
Yet slips away like grains on a beach.

Drifting Thoughts like Melting Snow

Thoughts like snowflakes gently fall,
Each one unique, they drift and stall.
As warmth approaches, they start to fade,
Leaving but memories, softly laid.

Whispers of winter, brief and bright,
Melt into moments, lost from sight.
Yet in their silence, beauty glows,
A fleeting glimpse, as the cold wind blows.

Whispers of Time

Time wanders softly, a ghostly breeze,
Carrying secrets through rustling trees.
Moments captured, then brushed away,
Echoes of laughter that silently stay.

A ticking clock holds dreams untold,
In shadows deep, the stories unfold.
Whispers weave through the fabric of night,
Illuminating all that's hidden from sight.

The Evaporation of Now

Now is a vapor, elusive and light,
Drifting away into the endless night.
Caught in the spiral of moments unclear,
Fleeting like dawn, it soon disappears.

Each heartbeat pulses in radiant glow,
Yet slips through fingers like grains of snow.
In the silence that follows, we breathe, we sigh,
For in this fleeting moment, we truly live high.

The Shortest of Stories

In whispers soft, a tale unfolds,
Of fleeting moments, love retold.
A glance exchanged under starlit skies,
Two hearts connected, no need for lies.

Yet time moves on, as shadows play,
And memories fade, like end of day.
But in the silence, their hearts still sing,
A timeless bond that love can bring.

Light's Quickening Dance

Beneath the moon, the shadows waltz,
As stars align, revealing faults.
The night gives rise to light's embrace,
A dance of flickers, a soft grace.

With every step, the spirits soar,
In twirls of splendor, forevermore.
The dawn awaits, with whispers bright,
As day awakens from the night.

Echoes of a Silent Heart

In quiet corners where dreams reside,
A silent heart learns to confide.
Every echo of a breathless sigh,
Carries the weight of a love gone by.

In the stillness, memories drift,
Each one a precious, fragile gift.
Yet time can mend what's torn apart,
Restoring hope in a silent heart.

When Time Embraces

In twilight hours, when time stands still,
Moments linger, and spirits thrill.
Each tick of the clock a tender sigh,
A dance with the past beneath the sky.

Fleeting seconds do intertwine,
With whispers of fate, so divine.
In the embrace of time's gentle arms,
We forge our dreams and weave our charms.

Sinking into Sweet Surrender

Close my eyes to the world,
Let the waves roll in.
Embrace the gentle pull,
Sinking deep, I begin.

Whispers of the sea call,
A lullaby in the night.
Each breath a soft retreat,
Into the depths of delight.

Floating on currents warm,
With every sigh I glide.
Letting go of my cares,
In this tranquil tide.

Here in this sweet surrender,
Time fades into the blue.
With the stars as my witness,
I welcome the calm and true.

Drifting Through Dimensional Dreams

In twilight's soft embrace,
I wander through the planes.
Colors swirl like whispers,
Each frame a new refrain.

Time bends and folds within,
As shadows dance and play.
Dimensions stretch and shimmer,
In subtlest shades of gray.

Voices echo softly,
In realms of mystic light.
I drift through endless spaces,
Bathed in moonbeam flights.

These dreams weave my journeys,
Through worlds yet unexplored.
Drifting on ethereal winds,
My spirit's gently soared.

The Art of Pause and Flow

In moments still and quiet,
I find the light within.
A gentle breath of nature,
As silence starts to spin.

The world rushes around me,
Yet here I take my stand.
With every pulse and heartbeat,
The universe at hand.

Letting go of the hurry,
Releasing every thought.
In the art of pause and flow,
Contentment is sought.

Time cascades like water,
With beauty in the slow.
In every cherished moment,
A peaceful heart will grow.

Timeless Fragments in the Now

Every second a treasure,
Each instant a gift.
In the tapestry of life,
We find our spirits lift.

Moments weave together,
Like threads in a loom.
In the fabric of existence,
We dance away the gloom.

Here in timeless fragments,
We learn to truly see.
In the beauty of the now,
We set our spirits free.

Embrace the fleeting shadows,
Honor dreams that you sow.
In the heart of each heartbeat,
Discover what is flow.

Echoes of Laughter

In the fields where children play,
Joy dances in the sun's soft ray.
Laughter rings like a sweet refrain,
Echoing softly in heart's domain.

Memories drift like autumn leaves,
Carried softly by gentle eves.
In every corner, happiness stays,
Painted in light of golden days.

Gone Too Soon

A fleeting glance, a whispered word,
Moments missed like songs unheard.
Time a thief in quiet night,
Taking dreams just out of sight.

With every tick, a story fades,
A heart once bright, now serenades.
Echoes linger, a soft tune,
Life's sweet melody gone too soon.

Whispers of Sugar on the Tongue

Sweet sensations dance in delight,
As dreams take flight in the quiet light.
Fingers trace on golden bliss,
Moments captured in a lover's kiss.

Life is richer in every bite,
Whispers linger in the soft night.
A sweetness shared, a tender song,
In every heart where it belongs.

Captured Fractions of the Find

In every glance, a treasure hides,
Fragments of joy like gentle tides.
Learn to see with open eyes,
Beauty often beneath the skies.

Tiny moments, they intertwine,
Glimpses of hope in every line.
Captured fractions, a gift so fine,
In little things, the stars align.

The Trickle of Well-Worn Wishes

With each new dawn, a wish is cast,
Old dreams echo, shadows of the past.
A trickle through the cracks of time,
Well-worn hopes in a simple rhyme.

Gentle whispers of what could be,
Flowing softly like a quiet sea.
Every wish, a story told,
In the heart where dreams unfold.

Shadows of Tomorrow

In the twilight's gentle sigh,
Whispers dance of dreams gone by.
Shadows stretch on paths untold,
Secrets of the night unfold.

Future waits in silent grace,
Each moment a fleeting trace.
Under stars that softly gleam,
Hope ignites in every dream.

Capture the Ephemeral

Time drips slowly from our hands,
Like grains of gold in shifting sands.
Catch the breeze, let moments flow,
In the now, let beauty grow.

Fragile petals in the light,
Fleeting glimpses, pure delight.
Hold them close, let laughter rise,
In the heart, the treasure lies.

Sunset's Soft Embrace

The sky blushes with evening's kiss,
A symphony of colored bliss.
Whispers of the day retreat,
Night wraps round with soft heartbeat.

Crimson clouds in amber hue,
Embracing dreams both old and new.
Nature hums a lullaby,
As the sun begins to die.

A Symphony of Seconds

Each tick of time, a note so pure,
Moments weave a tapestry sure.
Echoes of laughter fill the air,
Life's sweet song beyond compare.

Count the beats, a rhythmic dance,
In this life, seize every chance.
For in the seconds, stories bloom,
Creating light, dispelling gloom.

Stars in a Jar

Tiny lights in glass so clear,
Whispers of dreams that we hold dear.
Captured moments, night aglow,
Flickers of hope in the gentle flow.

Silent wishes, flickering bright,
Guiding us through the darkest night.
Each shine a story, each glint a song,
In this jar, we all belong.

Fragile treasures, memories spun,
Merging past with the present run.
A galaxy caught in fragile clasp,
In this small space, our futures grasp.

Stars in a jar, forever stay,
In our hearts, they light the way.
A universe held with gentle care,
Whispered secrets in the night air.

The Quiet Unraveling

In the stillness, threads unwind,
Echoes of thoughts left behind.
Moment by moment, peace takes flight,
Softly we face the fading light.

Whispers of time in gentle streams,
Fleeting shadows, fragile dreams.
Layers of silence, truth revealed,
In this quiet, hearts are healed.

Embers dance where shadows play,
An unraveling of light and gray.
Every heartbeat, soft and slow,
Drawing us closer to what we know.

The quiet whispers a tender balm,
In letting go, we find our calm.
With each unravel, we learn to see,
The beauty in simplicity.

Soliloquy of Seconds

Each second whispers, soft and low,
A soliloquy in ebb and flow.
Time stretches wide, then slips away,
In the dance of night and day.

Moments captured in a sigh,
Fleeting seconds, how they fly.
In the silence, stories blend,
Whispers of what does not end.

Ticking clocks, a steady beat,
Life unfolding, bittersweet.
Every heartbeat a poem spun,
In the race where we have run.

The soliloquy of life speaks true,
In every pause, a chance to renew.
Finding meaning as we embrace,
The cherished seconds we can't replace.

Breathing in the Breeze

A gentle sigh beneath the trees,
Nature's whisper, breathing ease.
Carried softly on the air,
Moments linger, free from care.

The world awakens, life anew,
In every gust, the heart breaks through.
Each breath a promise, light and free,
Flowing with grace, like the sea.

Rustling leaves sing songs of peace,
In the breeze, our worries cease.
Embrace the rhythm, flow like a stream,
In every breath, we find our dream.

Breathing in the breeze, we find,
The sweetest solace, unconfined.
As nature whispers, we align,
With the universe, pure and divine.

Fleeting Echoes

Whispers in the twilight glow,
Memories drift, soft and slow.
Shadows dance, a gentle trace,
Time's embrace, a fleeting space.

Leaves whisper as they fall,
Nature's grace, a silent call.
Moments fade, yet still we hold,
Echoes linger, tales retold.

Every heartbeat, time's caress,
In the stillness, we find rest.
Fleeting dreams on evening's tide,
In their wake, we softly glide.

Stars align in heavens bright,
Guiding us through endless night.
Fleeting echoes, memories dear,
In our hearts, forever near.

The Dance of Seconds

Ticking softly in the air,
Moments twirl without a care.
Every second, bold and free,
Invites us to dance with glee.

Footsteps echo on the floor,
Time, a partner we adore.
Round and round, the minutes play,
In this waltz of night and day.

With each tick, a story spins,
Life begins as music wins.
In the rhythm, feel the flow,
Time's sweet dance, a vibrant show.

The seconds shimmer, softly glide,
In their arms, we shall reside.
Together, lost in their embrace,
The dance of time, a sacred space.

Solstice of Serenity

Gentle light from sun's ascent,
Whispers of a day well spent.
Calm embraces, soul's delight,
As shadows wane with fading light.

In the stillness, thoughts align,
Nature's peace, a sacred sign.
Silence wraps the world in grace,
Solstice glimmers, time's embrace.

Golden hues of dusk descend,
Moments linger, hearts extend.
In this realm of quiet breath,
Solstice whispers life from death.

With the stars, we find our place,
In the night, a soft embrace.
Solstice of serenity,
Cradles dreams in harmony.

Heartbeats in Flux

In the rhythm of life's design,
Heartbeats dance, a sacred line.
Every pulse, a story told,
In the warmth, we feel the bold.

Changing tides, emotions rise,
In the depths, love never lies.
With each breath, we navigate,
Heartbeats guide us, love's own fate.

Moments shift like grains of sand,
Together, we will take a stand.
Through the storms and peaceful seas,
Heartbeats echo like the breeze.

In the flux, the truth we find,
Boundless love that intertwines.
With each heartbeat, we create,
A symphony that won't wait.

Fragile Moments

In the hush of twilight glow,
Time stands still, a gentle flow.
Whispers caught in trembling air,
Secrets shared, a bond laid bare.

Fleeting glances, soft and shy,
A spark ignites as days pass by.
Each heartbeat holds a story true,
In fragile moments, me and you.

The world outside can fade away,
While memories in shadows play.
Touch the edges of the night,
In fragile moments, we find light.

Hold them close, these tender tears,
Through the laughter, through the fears.
In every breath and sigh we take,
We cherish each, for love's own sake.

A Cascade of Laughter

Echoes dance on the summer breeze,
Laughter flows with effortless ease.
Joy spills over, bright and clear,
In every chuckle, every cheer.

Together we share secrets sweet,
With every joke, our hearts repeat.
A cascade of laughter, pure delight,
Illuminates the darkest night.

Bubbles rise in a sunlit stream,
Floating softly, like a dream.
Each giggle connects us more,
Holding joy we can't ignore.

In moments shared, our spirits lift,
Like playful waves, life's precious gift.
Let the laughter swell and soar,
A cascade of joy forevermore.

The Path of Softening

Along a winding, gentle trail,
Where whispered winds tell hidden tales.
Each step a choice, each turn a chance,
On the path where hearts may dance.

Tender leaves brush against the skin,
Embracing warmth from deep within.
A softening touch, a calming hand,
Guides us through this sacred land.

Sunlight dapples through the trees,
Setting souls at tranquil ease.
In every pause, a chance to grow,
The path of softening, hearts aglow.

Together we wander, hand in hand,
Through meadows bright and golden sand.
Embracing life's sweet harmony,
On this path, just you and me.

Ebb and Flow

Tides whisper softly to the shore,
Carrying dreams, forevermore.
Ebb and flow in rhythmic grace,
Life's dance unfolds in this embrace.

Ripples shimmer under the moon,
Every heartbeat sings a tune.
The waves might crash, then gently fade,
In ebb and flow, our fears unmade.

Moments rise like ocean spray,
Each sunrise brings a brand new day.
With every change, we learn to grow,
In love's embrace, we ebb and flow.

So let us ride this tide of time,
Through highs and lows, our spirits climb.
Hand in hand, we'll find our way,
In ebb and flow, come what may.

Drifting Through the Sand

Whispers of the wind hum soft,
Particles dance, aloft,
Footprints fade, time slips by,
Moments lost, as waves sigh.

Sunset drapes the hills in gold,
Stories of the sands retold,
With each grain, memories blend,
In the twilight, dreams extend.

Silhouettes of thoughts take flight,
Carried on the breeze at night,
Drifting where the heart recalls,
A thousand journeys in its thralls.

Endless paths beneath my feet,
Nature's rhythm, calm and sweet,
As I wander, freely roam,
In the sand, I've found my home.

Transient Bliss

Fleeting moments in the sun,
Laughter shared, two spirits run,
Each heartbeat a melodic tune,
In the arms of lazy afternoon.

Clouds drift by, like dreams untold,
Softly wrapped in warmth, they hold,
Wishes painted in the sky,
A canvas where our hopes can fly.

Time stands still, yet rushes past,
Memories weave, a tapestry cast,
In whispered tones, we find our way,
Grasping bliss that will not stay.

Twinkling stars by night's embrace,
Every glance, a loving trace,
In the ephemeral, we find rest,
Transient bliss, forever blessed.

Embracing the Sublime

Mountains rose to kiss the sky,
Majesty where eagles fly,
Nature's palette, bold and bright,
Invites the heart to seek the light.

Rivers hum a soothing song,
Flowing swift, yet where we belong,
Every drop a celestial dream,
Reflecting life's eternal stream.

Moments whisper through the leaves,
In their rustle, the spirit believes,
Embracing all that life can give,
In the sublime, we learn to live.

Stars ignite the velvet night,
Guiding souls with their soft light,
Together we learn to align,
In this vast world, your heart with mine.

The Tides of Transition

Waves crash down and pull away,
Like the thoughts we dare not say,
Each ebb and flow, a dance divine,
Embracing change like aged wine.

Seasons shift beneath our gaze,
Moments etched in timeless haze,
Paths diverge yet often meet,
In transitions, life is sweet.

A chrysalis in silent pause,
Emerging with a gentle cause,
Transformation is a sacred art,
Each ending leads to a fresh start.

Through the tides, we learn to trust,
In vulnerability, we find our rust,
Life unfolds, a journey grand,
Navigating through shifting sand.

Nature's Prelude

In the morning's tender light,
Birds awaken, take to flight,
Whispers of the rustling leaves,
Nature sings, the heart believes.

Softly petals start to bloom,
Gentle fragrance stirs the room,
Every stream and mountain high,
Echoes of the earth's soft sigh.

Clouds drift lazily above,
A symphony of peace and love,
Sunset paints the sky in hues,
Nature's palette, vibrant views.

Stars emerge in twilight's grace,
Worlds collide in vast embrace,
A reminder of what we find,
In nature's heart, our souls unwind.

Transitory Treasures

A fleeting glance, a whispered breeze,
Moments treasured, never freeze,
Sunrise touch on morning dew,
Life's embrace in every hue.

Time's hand moves, slow yet fast,
Echoes of a shadowed past,
Seasons change, like flowing streams,
Holding tight to fragile dreams.

Memory's dance in the twilight,
Fleeting moments, soft and light,
Each sweet laugh, a tender trace,
Transitory, yet full of grace.

Hold the now, let go the past,
Every heartbeat, joys amassed,
In the stillness, time will sing,
Life's true gift in everything.

Evaporating Whispers

Fog rolls in with morning's breath,
Silent secrets hide beneath,
Whispers linger, then they fade,
In the mist, new dreams are made.

Echoes hush in quiet morn,
Softly, as the day is born,
Words unspoken dance on air,
Evaporating, everywhere.

Each soft sigh, a fleeting kiss,
Moments like this, filled with bliss,
Shadows fade in golden light,
Whispers lost in taking flight.

Every glance, a story told,
Mysteries wrapped, yet unfold,
As the sun climbs ever higher,
Memories fade, like smoke, expire.

Dappled Time

Sunlight filters through the trees,
Dappled patterns, gentle breeze,
Hours drift like clouds above,
Time's embrace is soft, is love.

Shadows stretch across the glen,
Marking where the light has been,
Moments blend, a seamless song,
In this stillness, we belong.

Ticking clocks will always chime,
Yet we savor dappled time,
With each heartbeat, life we find,
Captured moments, intertwined.

Hold the laughter, catch the tears,
Paint the canvas of our years,
In the tapestry we weave,
Dappled time, we won't deceive.

The Heat of Existence

In the fire of life's embrace,
We dance with fleeting grace.
Moments flare and then expire,
As dreams ignite our inner fire.

Every heartbeat, every sigh,
Whispers truths that never die.
We seek in warmth a fleeting spark,
Illuminating paths through dark.

In the sun's eternal glow,
We feel the rhythm ebb and flow.
With each breath, a tale unfolds,
In the heat, our life beholds.

Through trials, joys, and endless quest,
We find what makes our souls rest.
In existence's vibrant play,
We cherish each and every day.

Chasing Celestial Shadows

Underneath the boundless sky,
We chase the stars, our spirits fly.
With every glance, the cosmos calls,
Where mystery and wonder sprawls.

In twilight's hush, we seek the light,
Chasing shadows into the night.
Galaxies swirl, their secrets deep,
In silence vast, our visions leap.

Each shooting star, a fleeting wish,
We dream of worlds with every swish.
Within the void, our hearts unite,
In celestial realms, we find our flight.

As comets blaze across the dark,
We find in stardust our own mark.
Through voids and spaces, we explore,
Chasing the shadows, forevermore.

Fleeting Fragments

Whispers of a bygone day,
In our minds, they gently sway.
Each memory, a precious thread,
Woven tightly, never shed.

Moments pass like shifting sands,
Through our grasp, like open hands.
In fragments lost, we seek to find,
The echoes of a wandering mind.

Fleeting glimpses, shadows play,
In the light of yesterday.
We chase the echoes, feel the pull,
In the depths, our hearts are full.

Each second spent, a treasure dear,
In the tapestry, we hold near.
Through the canvas of our plight,
Fleeting fragments dance in light.

Glinting in the Gloam

In the twilight's soft embrace,
We find our quiet, sacred space.
Here, the world begins to fade,
In gloaming light, dreams are laid.

Shadows stretch, and whispers sigh,
Beneath the vast and painted sky.
Each glimmer speaks of tales untold,
In the dusk, our hearts are bold.

Stars awaken, one by one,
In the dark, they dare to run.
Glistening hopes in silent streams,
Illuminating our hidden dreams.

As night descends, we breathe in deep,
In gloaming's arms, our secrets keep.
Through the dark, a light will beam,
Glinting softly in the dream.

Serenity in Surrender

In quietude, the heart finds peace,
As whispers of the soul release.
A gentle breeze, a soft embrace,
In surrender, we find our place.

The waves of life, they ebb and flow,
Accepting all, we start to grow.
With open arms, we greet the night,
In darkness, we discover light.

Let go of burdens, let time mend,
In stillness, learn that we can bend.
A tranquil mind, a steady hand,
In surrender, we understand.

Embrace the change, let go of fear,
In every loss, there's something near.
A serene heart, a clearer view,
In letting go, we are renewed.

Ephemeral Footprints

In the sand, we leave our trace,
A fleeting mark, a soft embrace.
With every wave that comes to shore,
Our memories fade, but love can soar.

Moments cling like morning dew,
Glistening bright, in shades of blue.
Each footstep tells a story bold,
Of laughter shared and tales retold.

Time's gentle hand will sweep away,
The paths we walked, the games we played.
Yet in our hearts, they still reside,
Ephemeral footprints, joy and pride.

Hold onto whispers of the past,
In every breath, those echoes last.
Though fleeting, love will always stay,
In cherished hearts, it finds a way.

Flickering Moments

A candle's glow in twilight's hush,
Fleeting seconds, emotions rush.
Each flicker tells a tale untold,
Of warmth and light, both brave and bold.

In laughter shared and silent sighs,
In every glance, the spirit flies.
Moments weave a tapestry,
Of life's sweet, brief mystery.

As shadows dance and dreams ignite,
We savor all, both day and night.
In flickers bright, our hearts align,
Each heartbeat, pulse, a cherished sign.

Embrace the now, let time be kind,
In fleeting space, your peace you'll find.
Hold dear the joy of every glance,
For in these moments, life will dance.

Glimmers of Tomorrow

Through cloudy skies, a light may break,
A hint of dawn, a promise make.
With every step, the future glows,
In glimmers bright, our courage grows.

Each star that twinkles in the night,
A spark of hope, a guiding light.
Like dreams that whisper in the breeze,
Tomorrow's wish, a heart that sees.

We chase the shadows, leave behind,
The burdens heavy on our mind.
With open hearts, we dare to dream,
In every thread, a hopeful seam.

So take my hand, we'll journey far,
In every moment, we are stars.
Together we'll create our path,
In glimmers of tomorrow's aftermath.

Sweet Release

In shadows deep, where silence breaths,
The burdens lift, like autumn leaves.
A gentle sigh, a whisper soft,
Embracing peace, the heart takes off.

The weight of days, like feathers drift,
Each moment's grace, a precious gift.
With open arms, the spirits soar,
In sweet release, we live once more.

Through tangled paths, we find our way,
A dance of light, in soft array.
With every tear, we cleanse the past,
In sweet release, we free at last.

The night gives way to dawn's embrace,
A canvas bright, a new-found space.
In every breath, a hope takes flight,
In sweet release, we find our light.

The Flickering Flame

In solitude, a candle glows,
Its warmth ignites, a soft repose.
Dancing shadows across the wall,
A flickering flame shall never fall.

In whispers low, the night unfolds,
Fables of love, the heart upholds.
With every flicker, dreams take flight,
A promise held in tender light.

When storms arise and darkness reigns,
The flame persists, despite the pains.
Through trials faced, it learns to thrive,
That flickering flame keeps hope alive.

As time drifts on, the glow will fade,
Yet in our hearts, the warmth is laid.
A beacon bright, in memories kind,
The flickering flame, forever aligned.

Yearning for Yesterday

The echoes call from times gone by,
In photographs where memories lie.
A lonesome heart, it aches and sighs,
For fleeting days that swiftly fly.

In whispered dreams, the past returns,
With laughter's spark, the heart still yearns.
Each fleeting glance, a cherished flame,
Yet time shifts on, it feels the same.

The seasons change, yet shadows stay,
In quiet moments, they softly play.
A melody of love once sung,
In dreams of youth, a song unsprung.

In hopes I find a whispered trace,
Of yesterday's sweet warm embrace.
Yet as I walk and time slips swift,
The yearning lingers, a cruel gift.

The Breath Between

In every pause, the silence sings,
A subtle space, where the heart clings.
Between the words, a promise made,
The breath between, forever laid.

A moment caught, a fleeting glance,
In tender stillness, souls may dance.
With every sigh, a world anew,
The breath between, where love shines through.

In whispered thoughts, the secrets flow,
In tranquil dreams, the shadows glow.
In every heartbeat's gentle sway,
The breath between shall lead the way.

So let us linger, not rush the time,
In tender rhythms, our souls align.
For in each pause, we truly see,
The breath between sets our spirits free.

Serendipity in Solstice Sunlight

In the golden hour's glow,
Whispers of fate gently flow.
Paths entwined beneath the trees,
Hearts unfold with tender ease.

Joy dances on the warm breeze,
Time slows down, as if to tease.
Moments captured, forever bright,
In serendipity's sweet light.

Shadows play and laughter rings,
Every glance a new beginning.
Sundrops fall like precious dew,
Every heartbeat feels brand new.

As the sun sinks low and deep,
In this magic, dreams we keep.
Solstice wraps us in its art,
With joy blooming in the heart.

Cascading Through Hours Unbound

Time slips softly like a stream,
Moments weave in endless dream.
Each second flows, a gentle sound,
In the laughter, life is found.

Waves of memory rise and fall,
Echoes of joy, a timeless call.
Drifting through the tapestry,
Unraveled threads of destiny.

Fleeting shadows, golden light,
Every hour, a new delight.
With each breath, the past dissolves,
In the now, our hearts resolve.

Cascading through this sacred time,
We dance to an endless rhyme.
In the river of today,
We find our bliss, come what may.

The Aroma of Dissolving Memories

Fleeting scents of days gone by,
Whisper softly, like a sigh.
Each fragrance holds a hidden tale,
In the air, their ghosts set sail.

Lingering warmth of summer nights,
Hopes entwined with city lights.
Sweet aroma of love's embrace,
In the heart, a sacred space.

Like perfume lost in twilight's hue,
Each memory, both old and new.
Dissolving slowly, yet profound,
In the stillness, peace is found.

Capturing what time won't hold,
Essence of us, stories told.
As the moments start to fade,
In the aroma, love won't jade.

Flickers of Glistening Bliss

Underneath the starlit sky,
Dreams ignite and softly fly.
Flickers dance on silver streams,
In the night, we find our dreams.

Whispers echo, hearts align,
In the darkness, stars will shine.
Glistening hopes in every breath,
In this moment, life feels fresh.

Each heartbeat sings a gentle song,
Together, we feel we belong.
Fleeting sparks of joy we chase,
In this dance, we find our place.

As dawn approaches, hues unfold,
Flickers fade, but dreams are bold.
In the light of morning's kiss,
We linger in our glistening bliss.

Embrace of Sunkissed Shadows

In the gold of morning's sway,
Shadows dance in bright array.
Laughter spills from trees that sway,
In their arms, we wish to stay.

Beneath the branches, secrets lie,
As whispers of the breezes fly.
Nature's heart beats soft and low,
In this warmth, we're free to grow.

Time drips like honey on our skin,
In the place where love begins.
Every glimmer, every smile,
Together lets our hearts beguile.

Embrace the light, let shadows play,
With every breath, we seize the day.
In the comfort of the sun,
We find our peace, our hearts as one.

The Linger of Twilight's Kiss

As the sun sinks with a sigh,
Colors swirl, the night draws nigh.
Stars awaken in the deep,
While the world begins to sleep.

Softly glows the evening light,
Whispers of the coming night.
Twilight wraps the earth in dreams,
Flowing softly like gentle streams.

Caught between the day and night,
Hearts aglow with soft delight.
In this moment, time stands still,
As we drink in evening's thrill.

Twilight's kiss, a tender grace,
In its arms, we find our place.
So let us linger, hand in hand,
Lost in twilight, love so grand.

Transforming Hues in the Air

Every dawn paints skies anew,
Pastels blend in vibrant view.
The brush of nature, bold and bright,
Ignites the heavens with pure light.

Leaves turn gold as breezes sigh,
Underneath the autumn sky.
Transforming shades of green and gray,
Nature's palette in disarray.

Flowers bloom in wild array,
Petals whisper, come what may.
Every hue a story speaks,
In the silence, beauty peaks.

In the air, the colors dance,
Each a spark, a fleeting chance.
Transforming hues, they evoke,
A magic world where dreams provoke.

Vast Horizons in Miniature

With each step, the world unfolds,
Tiny tales in whispers told.
Mountains rise in every grain,
Horizons vast in the mundane.

Little lakes reflect the sky,
In their depths, the wonders lie.
Every blade of grass holds dreams,
Vast as oceans, so it seems.

In the palm, a landscape small,
A universe that feels so tall.
In miniature, the heart explores,
Where tiny worlds open doors.

From the ant's quaint path we trace,
To the star's forgotten space.
Vast horizons touch the soul,
In each small piece, we find the whole.

The Weight of a Breath

In silent moments, we find our peace,
Each breath a whisper, a chance to cease.
The world fades softly, the noise subsides,
As we embrace what within us hides.

A heaviness lingers, yet feels so light,
Holding the stillness that dances at night.
With every inhale, a story unfolds,
The weight of a breath, more than what's told.

A fleeting moment, so fragile and rare,
Yet it carries dreams, a heartfelt flare.
In the depths of the heart, the essence grows,
The weight of a breath, only the spirit knows.

Surrendering to the Now

In the rush of time, we often forget,
To surrender our thoughts, to find our duet.
The moment is precious, a gift to behold,
In the arms of the now, true freedom unfolds.

Release all your worries, let silence reign,
In the gentle embrace, release the pain.
The past fades away, and the future is shy,
Surrendering to now, where true moments lie.

The heartbeat of life whispers soft and slow,
Carving paths through the unknown, we learn to flow.
Every breath a promise, every glance a vow,
In the sweetest surrender, we discover how.

Emblems of Ephemerality

A flower blooms bright, then quickly must fade,
An emblem of moments that life has portrayed.
Each sunset a canvas, each dawn a new start,
Reminding us gently of the dance in our heart.

The sparkle of dew, the flight of a bird,
Eclipses remind us, not all is assured.
In the laughter of children, the sorrow of tears,
We witness the beauty that spans through the years.

Emblems of life, so transient and sweet,
In every connection, our souls intertwine.
With gratitude whispered, we cherish each grace,
Knowing in moments, we find our true place.

Threads of Change

In the tapestry woven, our lives are aligned,
Threads of change linger, with purpose entwined.
Through valleys of struggle, we rise and we fall,
Every twist of fate, a chance to stand tall.

The colors of seasons seamlessly blend,
Reminding us softly, that nothing can end.
With courage in hand, we embrace the unknown,
Threads of change guide us, in wisdom we've grown.

Each fray tells a story, each knot brings us near,
The fabric of life, both precious and dear.
In the dance of creation, we find our own way,
Threads of change whisper, in light of the day.

Melted Seasons in Motion

Winter whispers softly, leaves descend,
A dance of frost, where time won't bend.
Spring rushes in with blossoms bright,
Colors awaken in the warm daylight.

Summer stretches, golden and bold,
Stories unfold in the heat, so uncontrolled.
Autumn sways with a gentle grace,
Nature's palette finds its place.

Winter will return with a chill embrace,
Yet in this cycle, our hearts find grace.
Seasons meld in a vibrant show,
A masterpiece that continues to grow.

In motion forever, time's sweet embrace,
Melted seasons in an endless chase.

Colors Blending in Warm Embrace

Red roses bloom, kissed by the sun,
While skies of blue invite everyone.
Golden hues dance on fields of green,
A vibrant canvas, nature's serene.

Orange sunsets, a day's sweet farewell,
Mingling colors in twilight's spell.
Purple dreams weave through night's gentle hand,
A tapestry woven across the land.

Colors blending, a warm embrace,
Every stroke tells of love and grace.
In this harmony, we find our place,
Lost in the beauty of time and space.

As the day fades, we open our hearts,
In this world of color, life never departs.

Tides of Now

Waves whisper secrets on the shore,
Each ebb and flow, a tale of yore.
Time dances in the salty breeze,
Carving memories with such ease.

Moments rise like the moonlit tide,
Cresting high, where dreams abide.
When shadows fall, the stars align,
In the ocean's heart, our souls entwine.

Rush of water, endless and free,
Learning from depths, just like the sea.
Each tide brings a reminder dear,
Of love, life, and what we hold near.

In the now, we find our way,
Guided by the light of the day.

Serene Adagio of the Heart

Soft notes drift in the evening air,
A gentle rhythm, a lover's prayer.
In quiet moments, hearts beat slow,
A serenade where emotions flow.

Whispers linger, sweet and light,
As shadows dance in the fading light.
Every sigh tells a story profound,
In this melody, love is found.

Time stands still, wrapped in grace,
Two souls move in this sacred space.
With each heartbeat, a tranquil art,
The serene adagio of the heart.

Lost in music, we drift away,
In symphonies of night, we sway.

Time's Gentle Caress

Time drifts softly, like a whisper,
Moments unfold with grace and ease.
Fleeting seconds, yet they linger,
In the heart, they leave their keys.

Shadows dance on walls of memory,
Each tick, a note in life's sweet song.
Holding hands with fleeting reverie,
In this moment, we belong.

As the sun dips low in the sky,
Golden hues paint the world anew.
With every heartbeat, we comply,
To the rhythm of what is true.

Seasons change, yet time remains,
A gentle touch, a warm embrace.
Through joys and sorrows, love sustains,
In time's caress, we find our place.

The Last Drop of Honey

Sweetness lingers on the tongue,
A taste of summer, pure delight.
Each last drop, a song unsung,
In twilight's glow, a soft respite.

Golden nectar, sun-kissed dreams,
Captured moments in a jar.
Life unfolds in gentle streams,
Where every breath feels like a star.

Memories cling like honey's trace,
Gentle whispers of what once was.
In every empty, sacred space,
Resides the warmth of love's applause.

So let us sip this nectar slow,
With every savor, life we glean.
For in each drop, sweet rivers flow,
The heart's secret, soft and serene.

The Softness of Here

In the hush of morning's light,
Gentle breezes brush the skin.
The world feels new, pure and bright,
In the soft arms of where we've been.

Petals fall like whispered dreams,
Colors dance in perfect cheer.
Every moment softly beams,
In the stillness, we draw near.

Leaves unfold with tender grace,
Each heartbeat a gentle sigh.
Here, we find our sacred space,
Beneath the vast and endless sky.

Let the whispers of today,
Embrace us in their warm embrace.
For in the softest hues, we play,
Finding peace in this shared place.

Advent of the Uncertain

A shadow lingers on the dawn,
Casting doubts amid the bright.
Hope treads softly, almost gone,
Navigating the edge of light.

Voices echo in the night,
Whispered dreams and hidden fears.
In this space of fragile light,
We confront our silent tears.

Yet within the fear resides,
A spark waiting to ignite.
In the unknown, courage hides,
Finding strength to face the night.

So let us walk this path unknown,
Hand in hand, we face the sway.
In the uncertainty, we've grown,
Through the dark, we'll find our way.

The Sweetness of Fleeting Moments

Time drips like honey, slow and sweet,
Memories linger, bittersweet and fleet.
Each laugh a treasure, tucked away tight,
In the shelf of the heart, a gentle light.

Seasons shift swiftly, like a whisper's call,
Moments cascade, like leaves they fall.
We savor the echoes, the joys that are gone,
In the tapestry woven, life marches on.

The sun dips low, painting skies aglow,
With colors of time, in a soft, gentle flow.
Embrace the now, for it slips away fast,
In the garden of life, we hold to the past.

In every heartbeat, in each fleeting glance,
We find the magic, the sweet, fleeting chance.
Dance to the rhythm, let moments take flight,
For in their embrace, our souls touch the light.

Merging Paths of Time and Taste

Two roads converging, a banquet laid wide,
Flavors entwined, where our senses collide.
Savory whispers of journeys we share,
In the realm of our stories, rich and rare.

A sip of nostalgia, a bite of the now,
In the feast of our lives, we savor each vow.
Memories seasoned with laughter and cheer,
Raise a glass to the moments we hold dear.

Candied dreams linger, sweet on the tongue,
As we weave through the hours, forever young.
With every morsel, a tale to unfold,
In the kitchen of life, we're brazen and bold.

The spices of fate, the blend of our days,
Crafting connections that in warmth always stays.
In a dance of flavors, we find our grace,
In merging the past, the present finds place.

Fluidity of the Present Pulse

The river of time flows, a dance so profound,
In the here and the now, our spirits are bound.
With every heartbeat, a wave in the sea,
The essence of living, a fleeting decree.

Moments collide like waves on the shore,
Bringing whispers of now, forevermore.
The pulse of existence, a rhythm in sync,
Drawing us closer, like thoughts in a blink.

What glimmers today may fade into mist,
Yet each fleeting moment is a pearl in the tryst.
Embrace the fluidity, the ebb and the flow,
For life's gentle currents will shape how we grow.

Through shadows and sunlight, we dance in the light,
With every heartbeat, the world feels just right.
In the fluid embrace of the present we thrive,
In the pulse of existence, we learn to survive.

Embracing Change like Warm Rain

Soft droplets fall, wrapping the earth,
A gentle reminder of nature's rebirth.
With every change, a new canvas appears,
Washing away worries, dissolving our fears.

Like warm summer rain, life showers our way,
Cleansing the pain, ushering a new day.
Embrace the unknown, let go of the old,
In the dance of transition, we gather the bold.

The wind carries whispers, a tale to unfold,
Of moments transformed, of lives to behold.
In the storm of our journeys, we stand side by side,
With hearts open wide, in the soft, flowing tide.

Let the warmth of the rain wash over your soul,
Embracing the change, we become truly whole.
For in every downpour, life's beauty resides,
In the dance of the moments where our spirit abides.

Fleeting Echoes of Time

Time slips through our fingers,
Like sand in an hourglass.
Memories fade, yet linger,
In shadows of moments past.

We chase the fleeting whispers,
Of laughter and love's caress.
Each heartbeat a reminder,
Of life's sweet, transient mess.

The clock ticks on, relentless,
As days slip into the night.
We grasp at what's defenseless,
In the dance of pale moonlight.

Yet in the depths of silence,
Echoes of joy remain.
A melody of existence,
Sings softly through the pain.

Whispers of Ephemeral Days

Morning dew on petals,
Like gems upon the grass.
Each day a fleeting canvas,
Brushed with colors that pass.

The sun rises in splendor,
A fresh and golden hue.
Yet twilight whispers softly,
Its shadows bid adieu.

Moments slip like water,
Through hands that grasp in vain.
We dance with soft uncertainty,
In sunlight and in rain.

As evening falls around us,
We gather what we've sown.
In whispers of the twilight,
We find the seeds we've grown.

The Dance of Liquid Shadows

A ripple across the surface,
Echoes of what was there.
Shadows sway in silence,
With a grace beyond compare.

Reflections weave their stories,
In the twilight's gentle gleam.
Every pulse tells a secret,
Beneath the moon's calm beam.

We twirl in soft illusions,
Caught in twilight's embrace.
Time dances with the shadows,
A fleeting, fickle chase.

Yet in this soft ballet,
We find a glimmer of truth.
These shadows hold our essence,
In memory's fleeting youth.

Transient Glimmers of Light

Stars flicker in the darkness,
Distant dreams that spark the night.
Each glimmer tells a story,
Of paths that sought the light.

The sunset bleeds its colors,
Across the canvas of the sky.
As day gives way to twilight,
We watch the moments fly.

In whispers of the evening,
Glimmers dance in the air.
Transient tales of longing,
Fleeting whispers of care.

Embrace the soft illumination,
Let shadows play their part.
For in these fleeting glimmers,
Lies the essence of the heart.

The Sway of Shadows

In the twilight's gentle embrace,
Whispers of dusk softly trace,
Figures dance in muted gray,
Night's secrets begin to sway.

Beneath the trees, shadows creep,
In silent grace, they softly leap,
Stories woven in fleeting light,
Echoes of the day take flight.

The moon hangs high, a watchful eye,
Casting dreams as time drifts by,
With every breath, the night unfolds,
In the heart of shadows, truth beholds.

A tapestry of dark and bright,
The swaying forms, a ghostly sight,
In the quiet, life shall blend,
Shadows whisper, never end.

Luminescence of Loss

In the quiet of the night,
Memories flicker, faint light,
Echoes of laughter still remain,
A heart wrapped tight in sweet refrain.

Through the silence, tears do flow,
In each heartbeat, the shadows grow,
Yet from the darkness, soft glimmers shine,
Whispers of love, eternally mine.

The stars above, a reminder soft,
That all we cherish is never lost,
In the folds of time, we seek and find,
The luminescence left behind.

Though absence lingers like a sigh,
In every moment, love won't die,
For in the void where silence lies,
The light of loss forever flies.

The Escape of Essence

Through the maze of fleeting days,
Essence waltzes, softly sways,
Glimmers caught in the morning dew,
Moments rise, then fade from view.

In the stillness of the dawn,
Time slips past, the veil is drawn,
Fragments of a life once known,
Drift like seeds that have been sown.

The laughter carried on the breeze,
Permeates through the swaying trees,
In every whisper, the spirit soars,
Essence escapes, forever roars.

Caught between the now and then,
Where memories live and breathe again,
With every heartbeat, truth unfurls,
The essence dances, touching worlds.

Momentary Rhapsody

In a fleeting, tender glance,
Life ignites in a vibrant dance,
Colors burst in a symphony,
An echo of sweet harmony.

Every heartbeat, a spark of flame,
Moments lost yet never tame,
In joy's embrace, we seize the day,
A rhapsody that fades away.

Through laughter's light, we find our way,
In the echoes of what we say,
With each note, the heart takes flight,
Captured in the glowing light.

Though brief, this joy we cannot hold,
A treasure more than gems of gold,
For in the dance, we come to know,
Life's rhapsody, a fleeting glow.

Fragments of Forever

In whispers soft, the shadows play,
Each memory lingers, fading away.
Time dances lightly on fragile wings,
Collecting moments, and all that life brings.

Beneath the stars, where silence dwells,
The heart keeps secrets that only it tells.
Fragments of laughter, tears from the past,
In the tapestry woven, memories last.

Through the corridors of dreams we roam,
Finding pieces of the heart that feels like home.
In every heartbeat, a story unfolds,
Of love and loss, of warmth and of cold.

So cherish the fragments, hold them near,
For in every moment, we conquer our fear.
Life's fleeting beauty, a treasure we hold,
In fragments of forever, our stories are told.

The Art of Letting Go

In whispered breezes, the past drifts away,
Like autumn leaves in the sunlight's sway.
Embrace the change as seasons unfold,
The art of letting go is a story retold.

Each memory cherished, a lesson once learned,
In the quiet spaces, a new path is turned.
With every goodbye, a chance to renew,
In the dance of release, find freedom to pursue.

The weight of our burdens can soften, can fade,
As we learn to trust in the choices we've made.
Let the tides carry away what we know,
In the journey of life, there's beauty in flow.

So lift up your heart to the skies overhead,
For in letting go, new dreams can be fed.
With grace in our steps and hope in our soul,
The art of letting go makes us whole.

Cascade of Dreams

In the twilight glow, where wishes collide,
A cascade of dreams begins to reside.
Flowing like rivers, they twist and they twine,
A symphony played on the heart's fragile line.

Each dream a lantern, alight in the dark,
Illuminating paths where our passions embark.
With colors of hope, they shimmer and gleam,
A vibrant reminder of life's vivid stream.

Through valleys of doubt, they whisper and sing,
In the silence of night, our aspirations take wing.
The cascade of dreams, an endless embrace,
A journey that fills with each daring trace.

So let us keep dreaming, with courage we climb,
For the cascade of dreams dances through time.
In every heartbeat, a promise reclaims,
The beauty of life in its wild, precious frames.

When Moments Flee

In fleeting seconds, our lives intertwine,
Moments like whispers, so hard to define.
They flicker like fireflies, bright in the night,
Illuminating paths with their soft, gentle light.

When laughter erupts and shadows are cast,
Each second a treasure, yet never can last.
Like waves on a shore, they ebb and they flow,
In the dance of existence, we learn to let go.

Through the laughter and tears, in joy and in pain,
We grasp at the moments, like drops of the rain.
For when moments flee, they leave traces behind,
A tapestry woven, our hearts intertwined.

So cherish them dearly, these whispers of time,
In the rhythm of life, let your spirit be prime.
In the beauty of chaos, when moments take flight,
Remember them fondly, like stars in the night.

Milton Keynes UK
Ingram Content Group UK Ltd.
UKHW022223251124
451566UK00006B/90

9 789916 906682